Swearing Santa

SwearWord Adult Coloring Book

ButtFiend

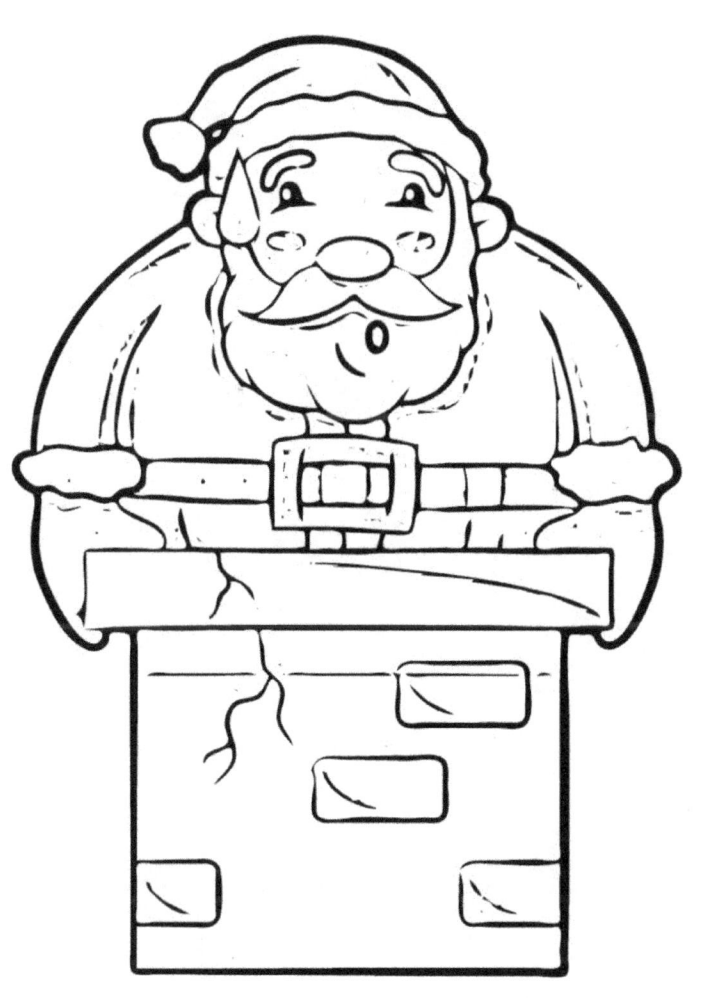

Schlong

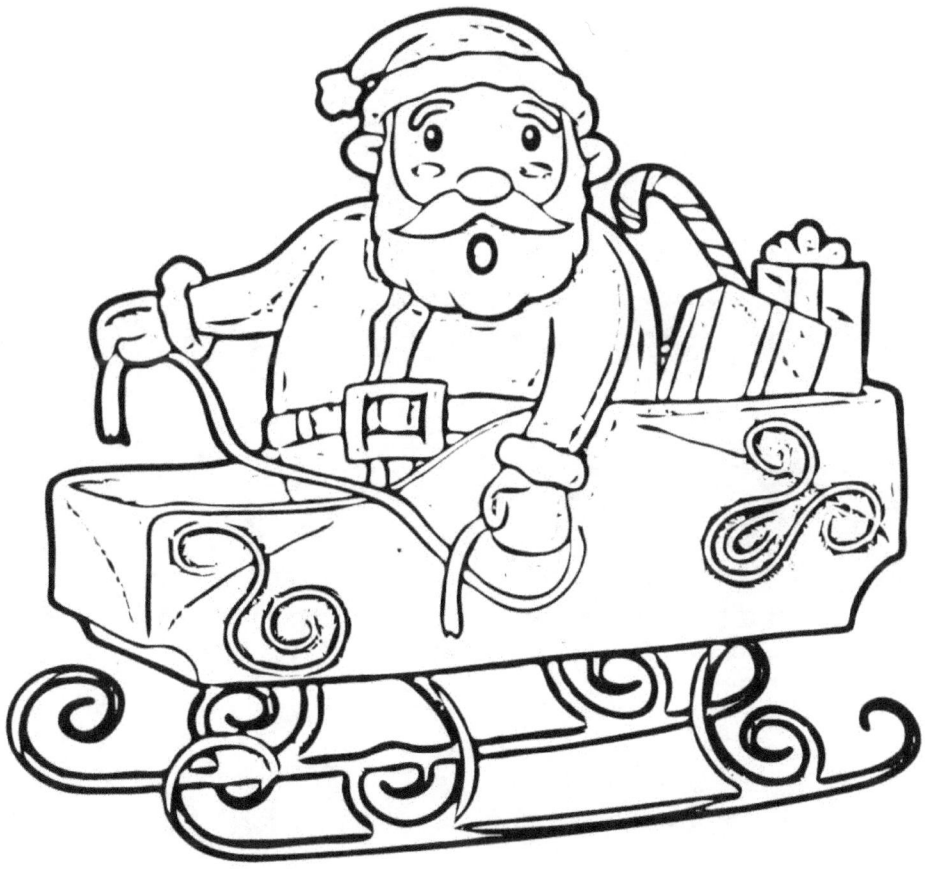

TwatCake

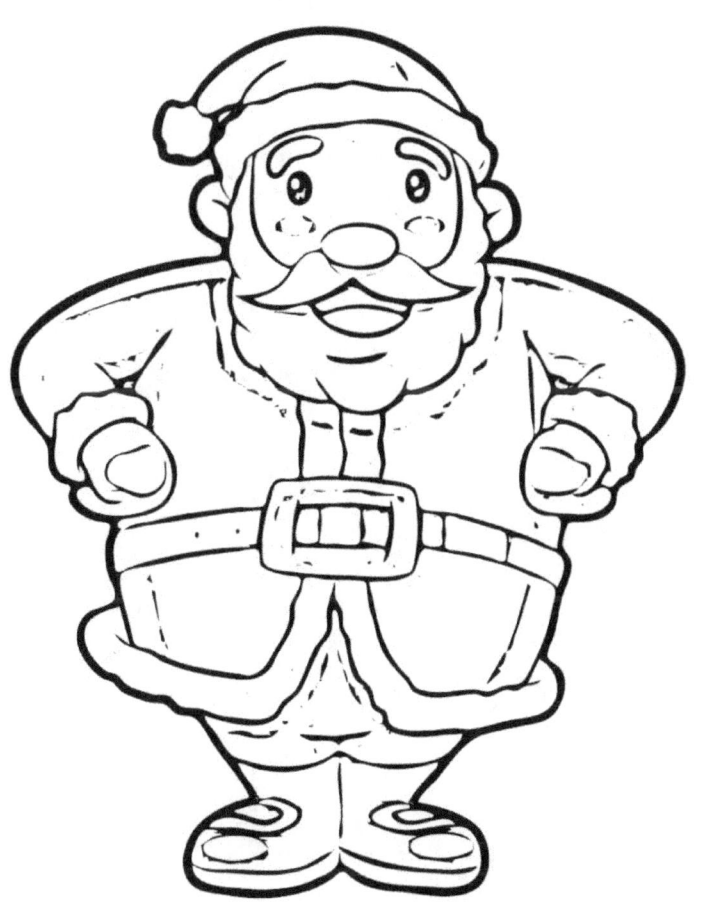

KnobWad

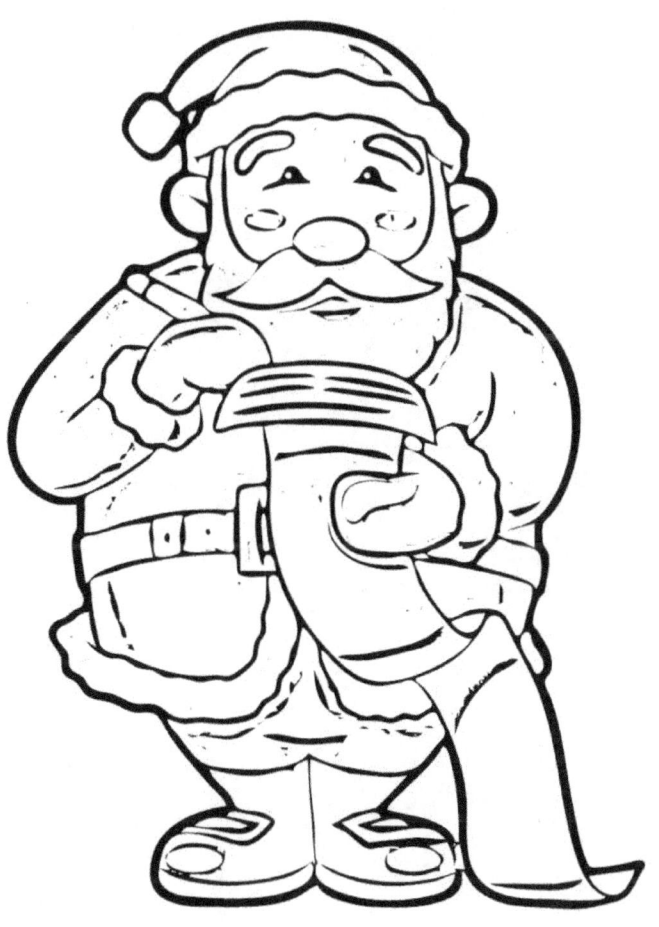

TrannyTug

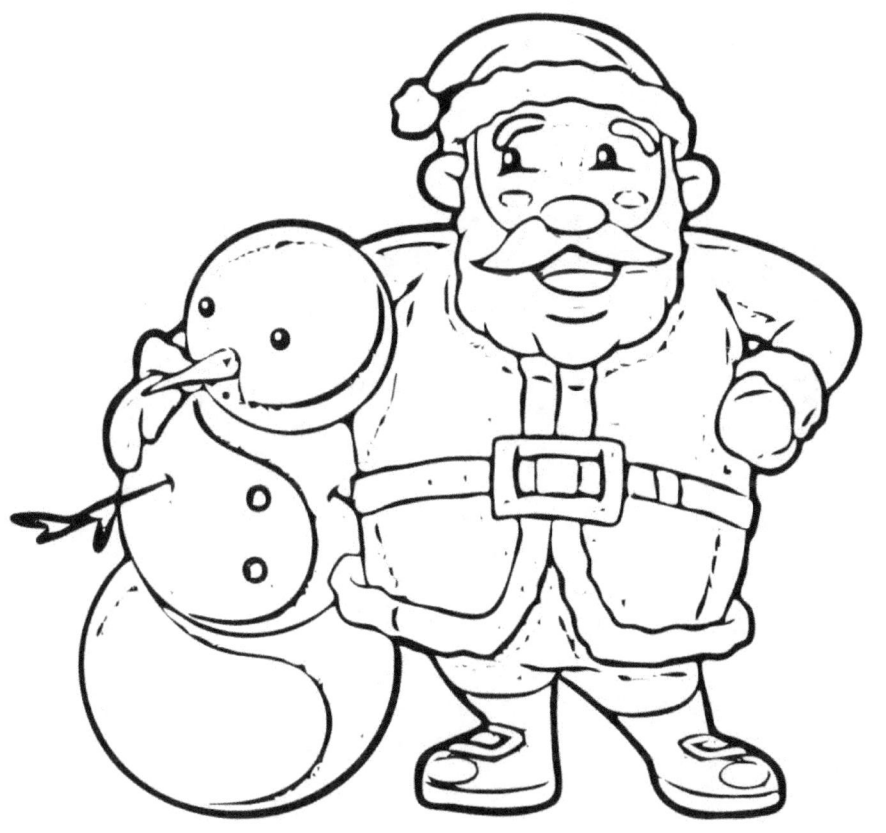

CrapFace

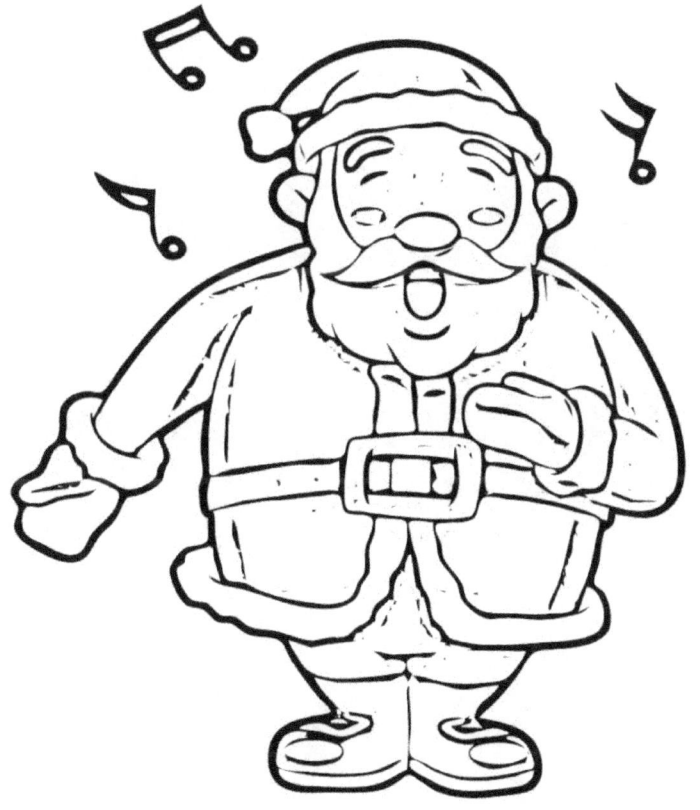

CockSack

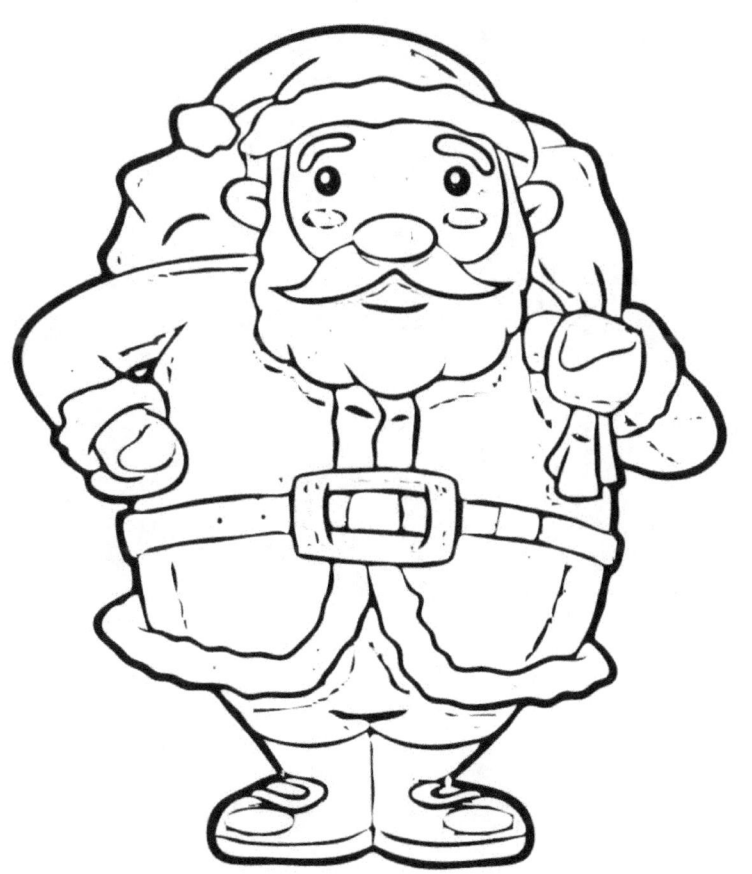

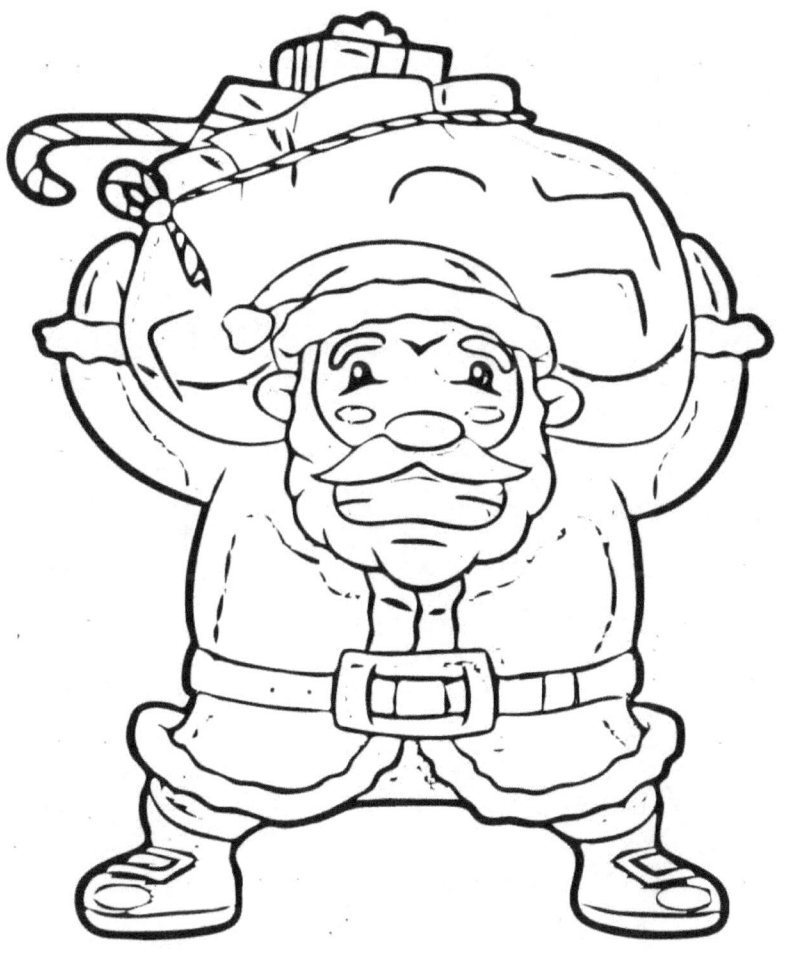

AssHat

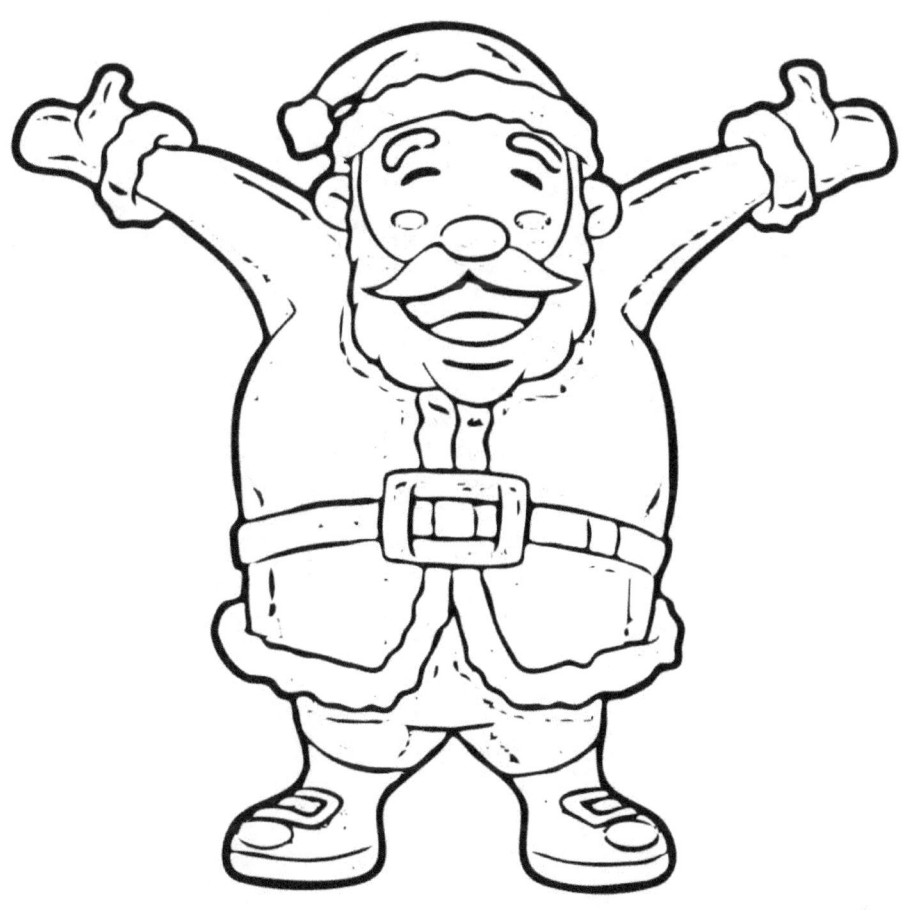

Balls

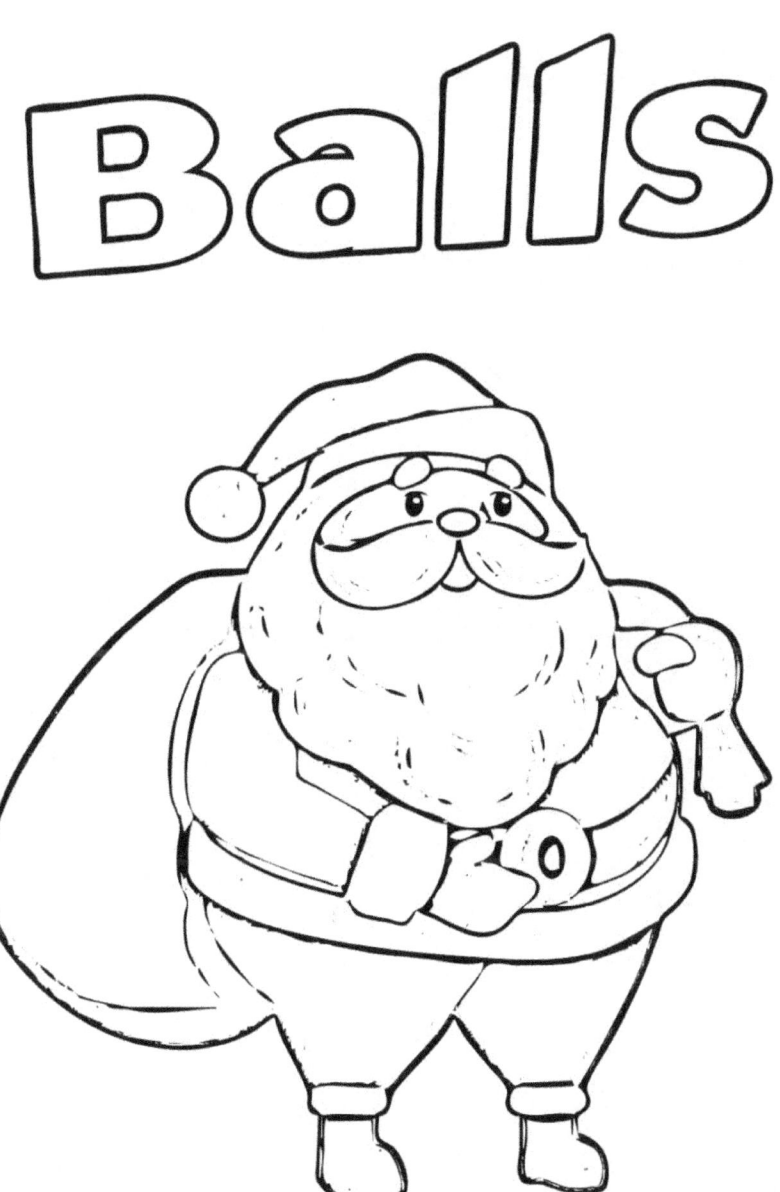

WankStain

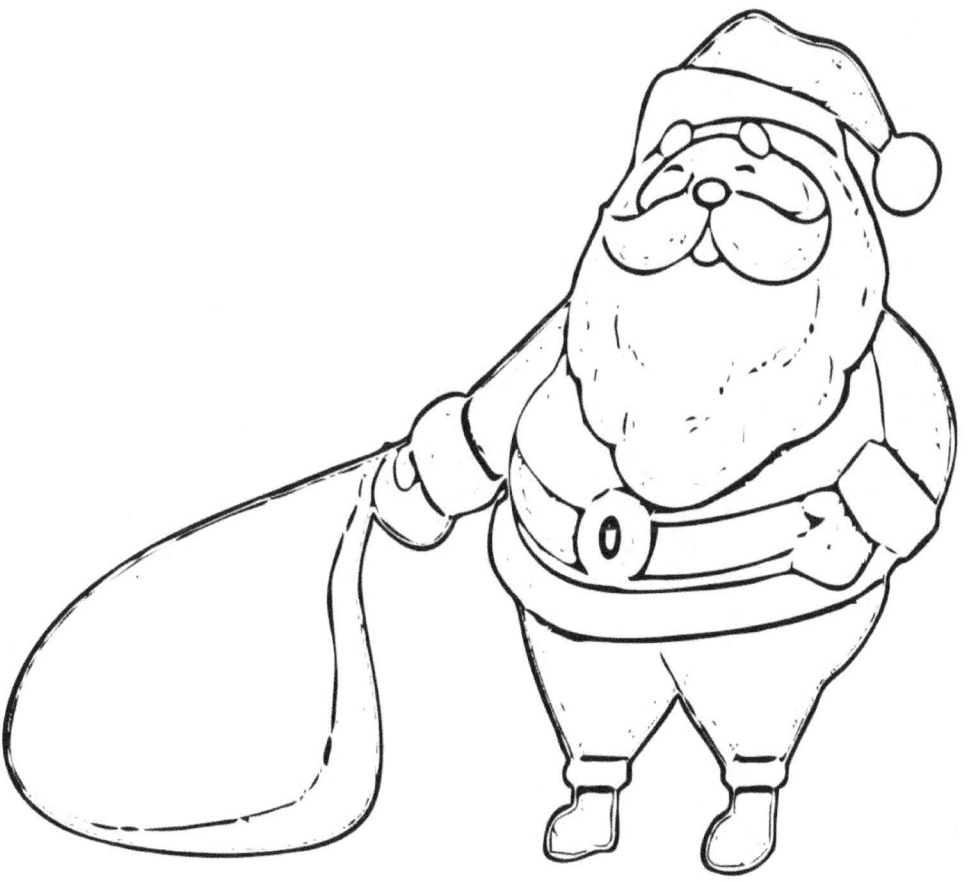

GutterHo

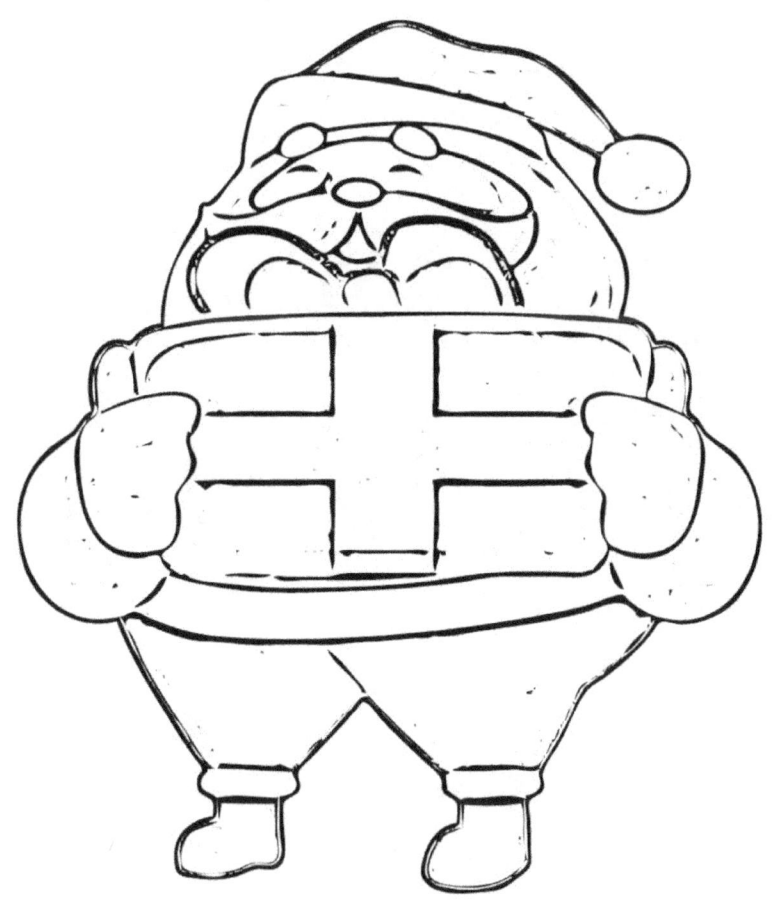

Wanger

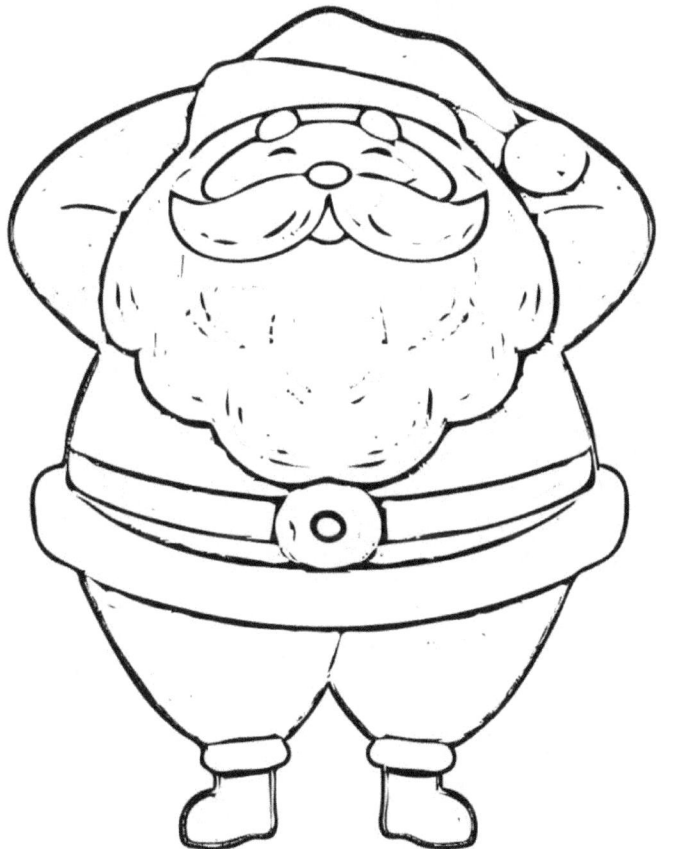

Bastard

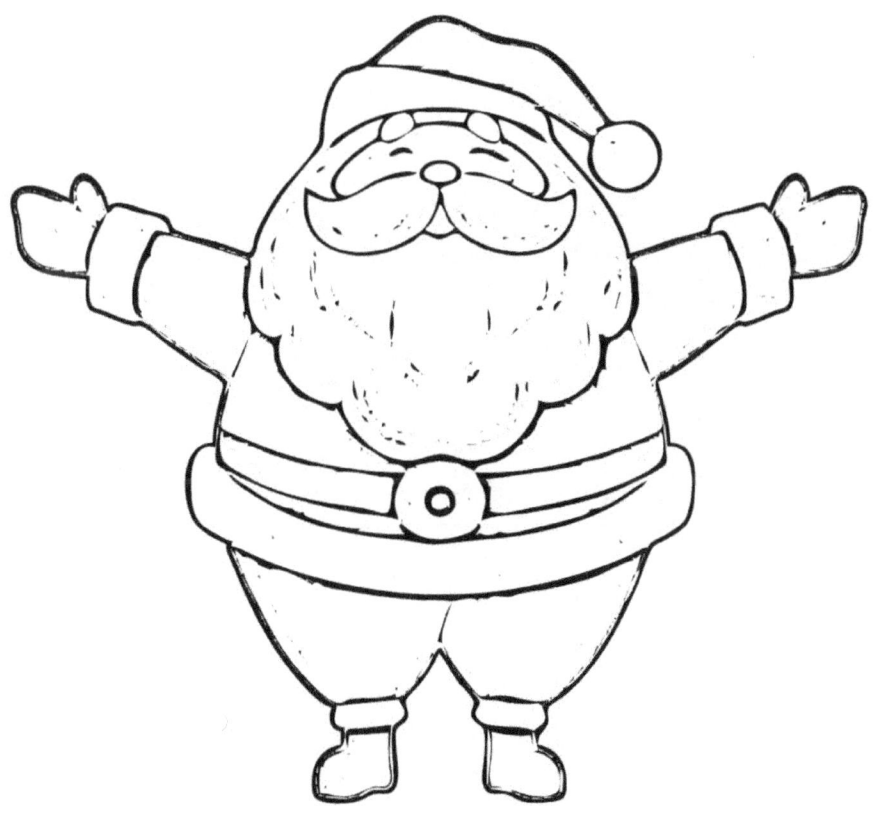

SuckMeDry

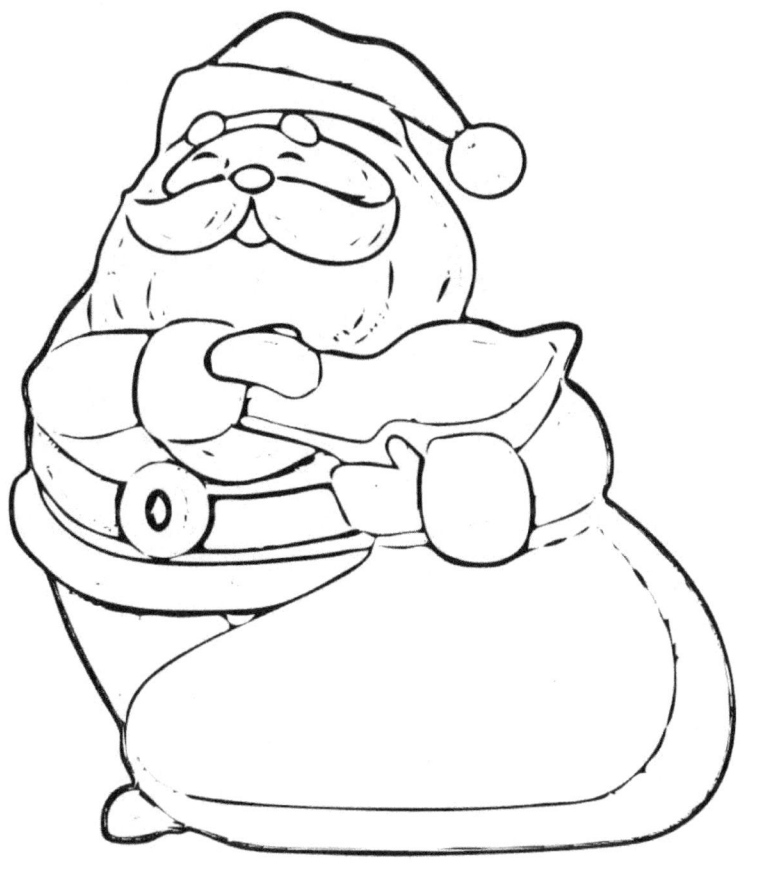

Tits

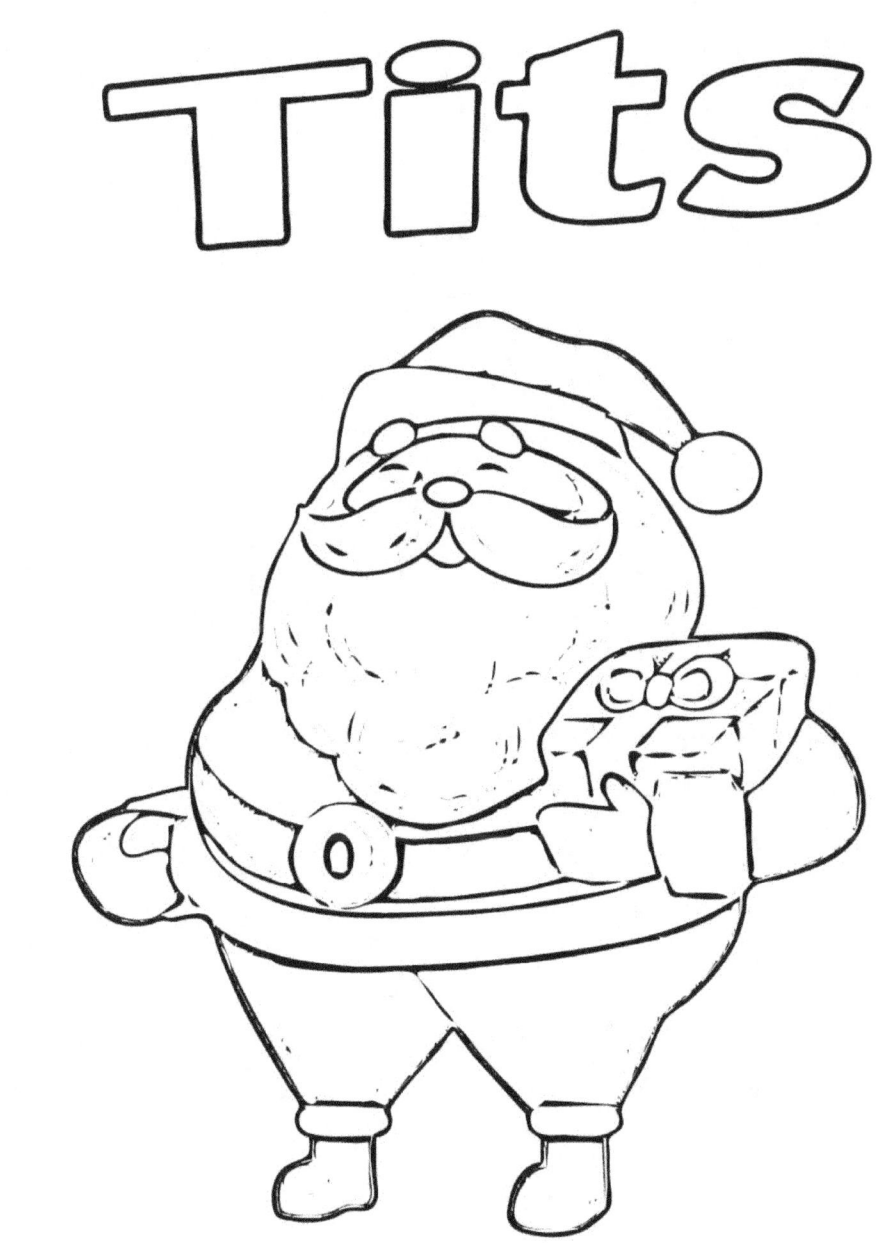

BigNuts

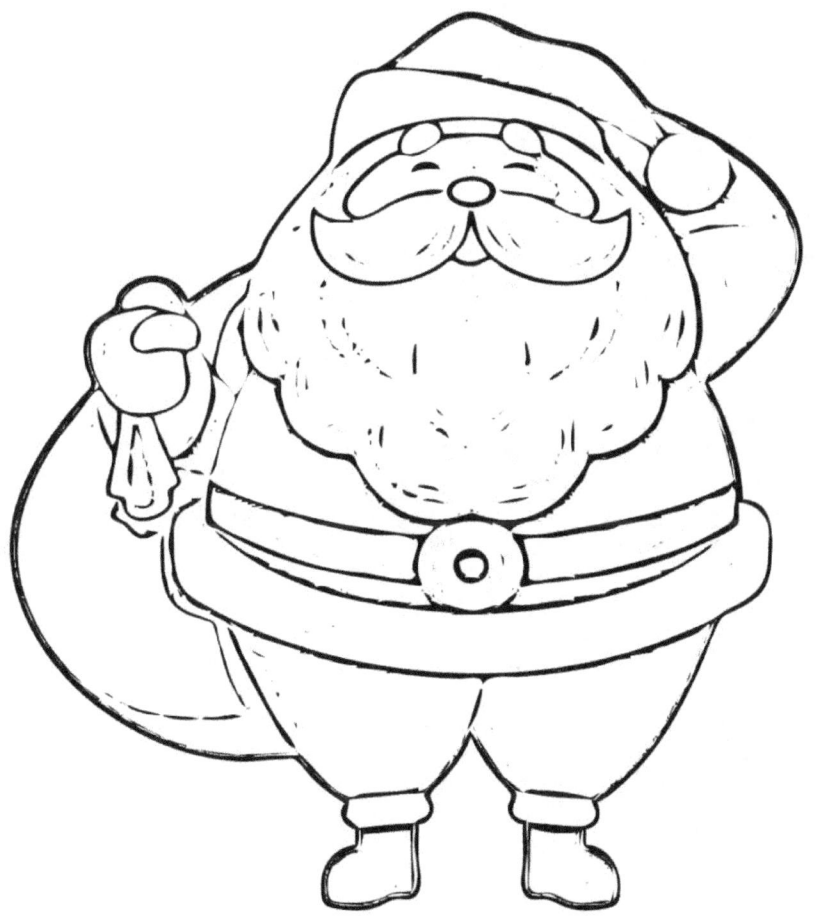

SlutBag

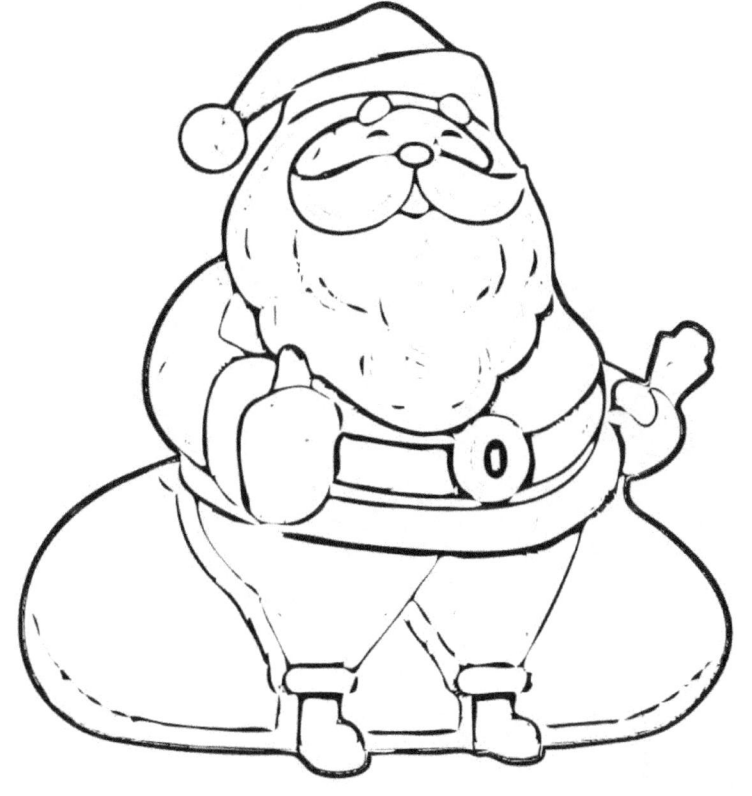

AssMunch

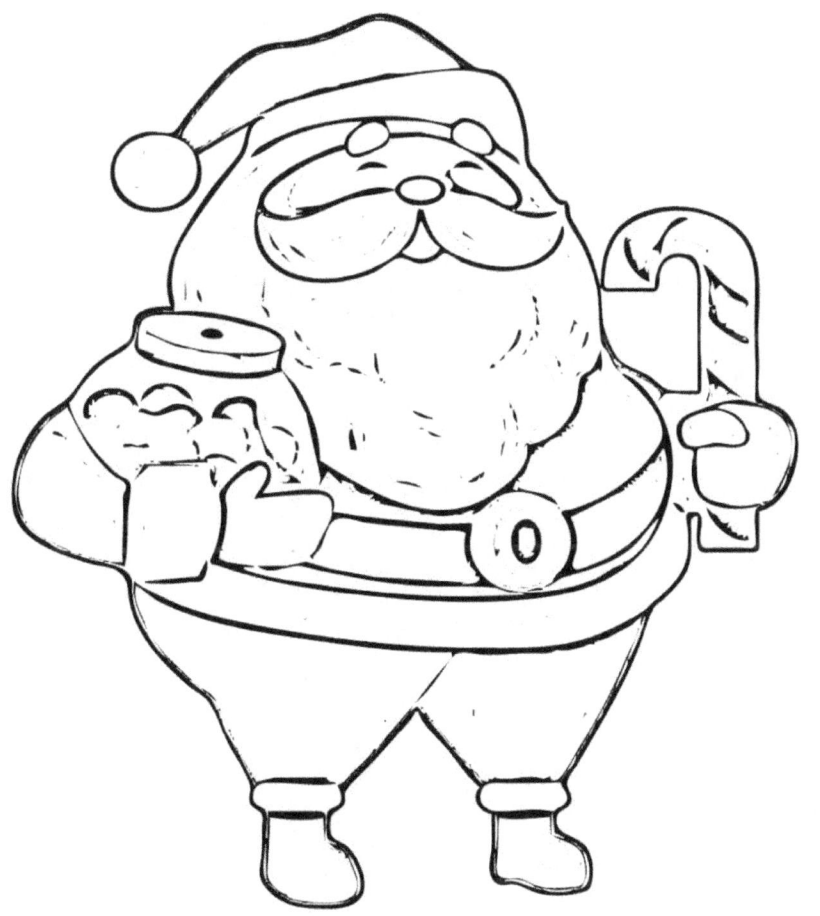

DickPipe

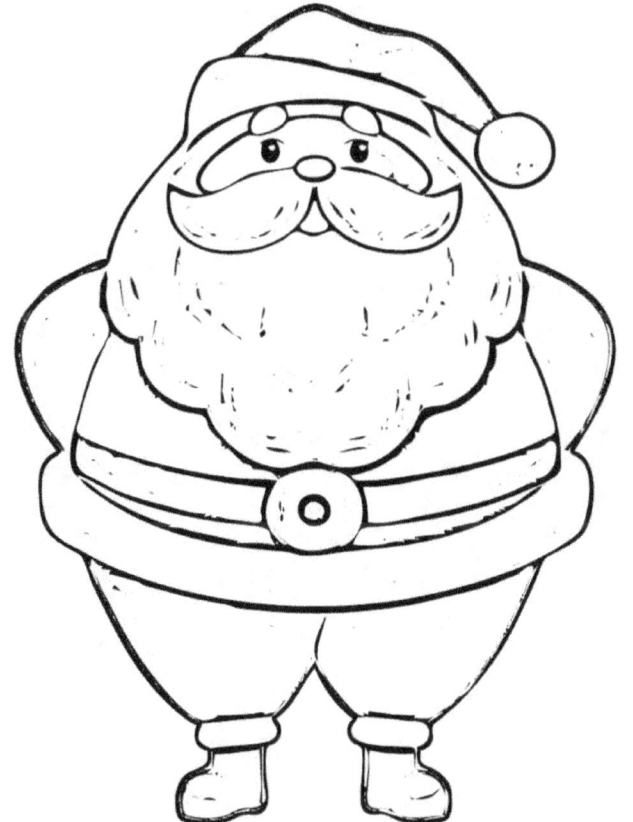